6
John Quincy Adams
1825–29
7
Andrew Jackson
1829–37
8
Martin Van Buren
1837–41
9
William Henry Harrison
1841
John Tyler
1841–45
MW00637874
16
Abraham Lincoln
1861–65
17
Andrew Johnson
1865–69
18
Ulysses S. Grant
1869–77
19
Rutherford B. Hayes
1877–81
20
James A. Garfield
1881
27
William Howard Taft
1909–13
28
Woodrow Wilson
1913–21
29
Warren G. Harding
1921–23
30
Calvin Coolidge
1923–29
31
Herbert Hoover
1929–33
37
Richard M. Nixon
1969–74
38
Gerald R. Ford
1974–77
39
Jimmy Carter
1977–81
40
Ronald Reagan
1981–89
41
George H. W. Bush
1989–93

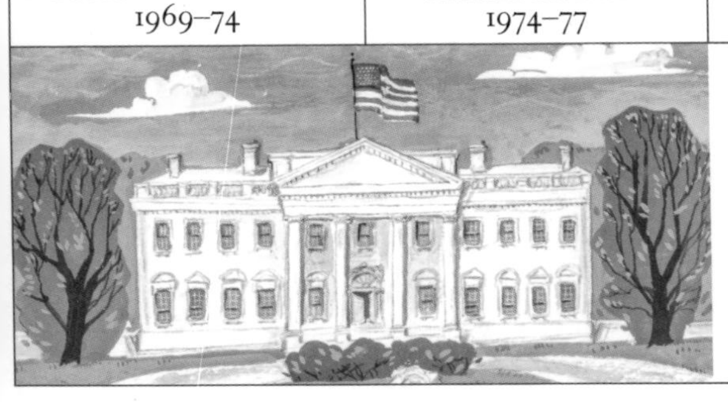

THE WHITE HOUSE HAS BEEN THE HOME AND OFFICE TO EVERY PRESIDENT OF THE UNITED STATES SINCE JOHN ADAMS.

Gigi at the White House!

Text by **Giovanna McBride** • Illustrated by **John Hutton**

THE WHITE HOUSE *HISTORICAL ASSOCIATION*

Laura Bush

Dear Readers,

One of the highlights of living in the White House is welcoming visitors from around the world. President Bush and I also looked forward to hosting the families of the people who worked at the White House and getting to know their children.

Giovanna McBride, or "Gigi" as we call her, first visited the White House a few days after we moved in. She was only six months old. Eight years later, when our time in Washington had come to an end, Gigi had grown into an active little girl, eager to explore the People's House.

I am thrilled she has taken her special experience and shared it with you in this wonderful book. I hope you will enjoy exploring the White House with Gigi—visiting the Oval Office, the bowling alley, the pool, and the movie theatre. And imagine what it would be like to watch fireworks on the South Lawn, Trick-or-Treat with a President, or meet Santa in the Blue Room at Christmas time.

Gigi had many memorable experiences at the White House, and I invite young readers to join her for this fun adventure.

Happy reading!

Laura Bush

When I was a little girl, my mom worked for First Lady Laura Bush in the White House—sometimes I would visit!

Once after a fun sleepover, Mrs. Bush invited me to eat breakfast with her.

Watching the tourists from the kitchen window, she asked what my favorite memories were. Let me tell you about my favorite things . . .

My Mom's Office

Sometimes I sat at my mom's desk and pretended to make very important calls.

The Secret Service Agents

The agents let me borrow their sunglasses so I could look like them.

The Movie Theater

The Movie Theater has big red velvet chairs and you can eat popcorn!

The Bowling Alley

The ball was heavy but it was still fun to bowl!

The Dogs

I got to play with the dogs, Barney and Miss Beazley, in the East Garden.

The Pool

One hot summer day I cooled off
and splashed around in the pool.

Summer Picnics

I rode merry-go-round horses and real horses at the special picnic for members of Congress!

The Fourth of July

There is no place more fun than the White House Lawn for watching fireworks.

The Pastry Chefs

At Christmas, the White House Pastry Shop is famous for building an entire "White House" out of gingerbread!

The Flower Shop

Sometimes I helped the florists arrange the beautiful flowers.

The Guests

I met Olympic swimmers,
gymnasts, and soccer players
and got to try on a Gold Medal. . . .

. . . Once I even saw Queen Elizabeth II of England at the White House!

Halloween

I went trick-or-treating to all the offices at Halloween.

Christmas

And I visited Santa when he stopped by the Blue Room.

Easter Monday

At the Easter Egg Roll, there was a hunt for the golden egg, face painting, a petting zoo, and the Easter Bunny gave us carrots.

The Helicopter

One special day my kindergarten class came to see the president fly away in *Marine One*!

The Press Room

I needed a stool to see over
the podium in the Press Room.

The Oval Office

I thanked President George W. Bush for all the fun times I had at the White House.

I told Mrs. Bush that with so many great memories, there could never be just one favorite thing! The first lady smiled and I said "Wow! I'm one lucky girl."